Piano Recital Showcase

SUMMERTIME FUN

12 FAVORITE PIECES
CAREFULLY SELECTED FOR ELEMENTARY LEVEL

CONTENTS

ISBN 978-1-4234-9590-1

HAL•LEONARD®
CORPORATION

7777 W. BLUEMOUND RD. P.O. BOX 13819 MILWAUKEE, WI 53213

In Australia Contact:
Hal Leonard Australia Pty. Ltd.
4 Lentara Court
Cheltenham, Victoria, 3192 Australia
Email: ausadmin@halleonard.com.au

Visit Hal Leonard Online at
www.halleonard.com

The Enchanted Mermaid

By Jennifer Linn

Magically singing (♩ = 84)
Play both hands one octave higher throughout.

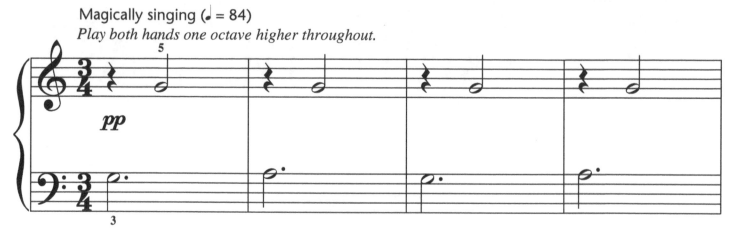

Hold down damper pedal throughout. (Solo)

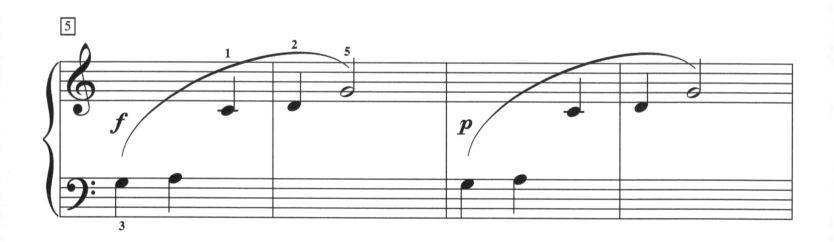

Accompaniment (Student plays one octave higher than written.)
Magically singing (♩ = 84)

With pedal

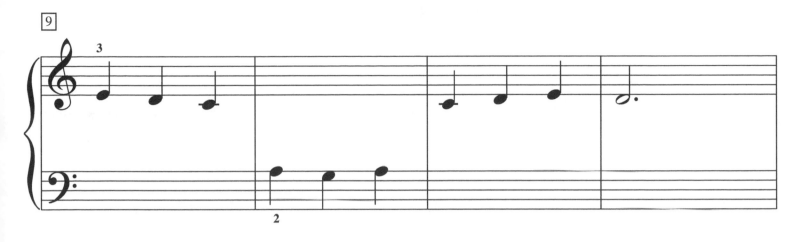

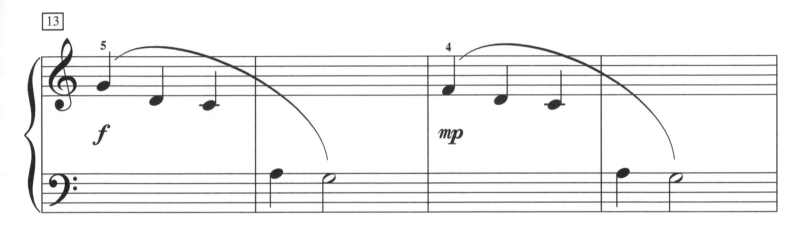

Missing You

to my "Lullaby Angel"

By Phillip Keveren

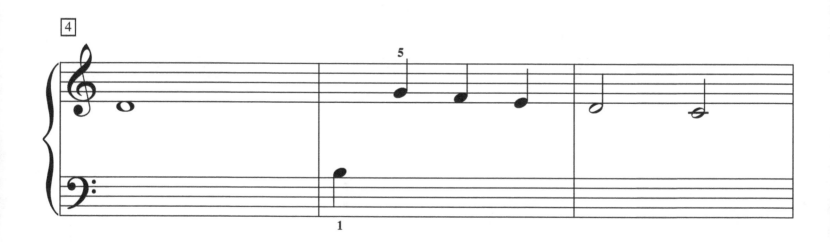

Accompaniment (Student plays one octave higher than written.)

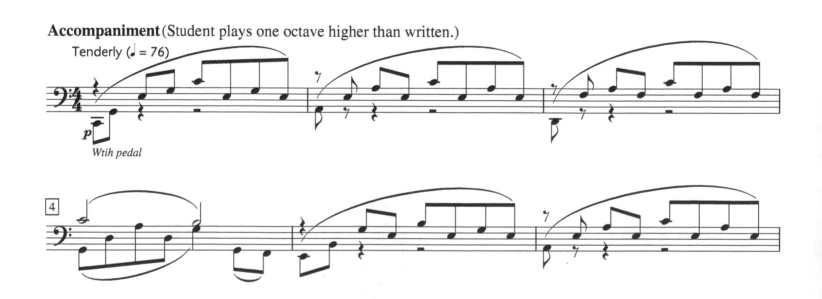

Butterflies and Rainbows

Words and Music by
Jennifer Linn

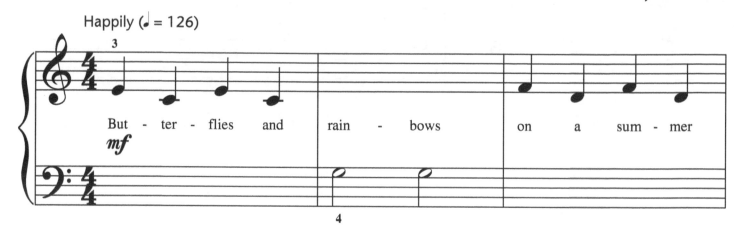

Butter-flies and rain-bows on a summer day. Happy things are special when they

Accompaniment (Play one octave higher throughout.)

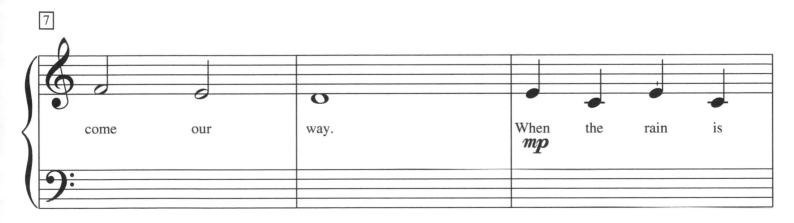

come   our   way.   When   the   rain   is

fall   -   ing,   and   you're   feel   -   ing   blue,

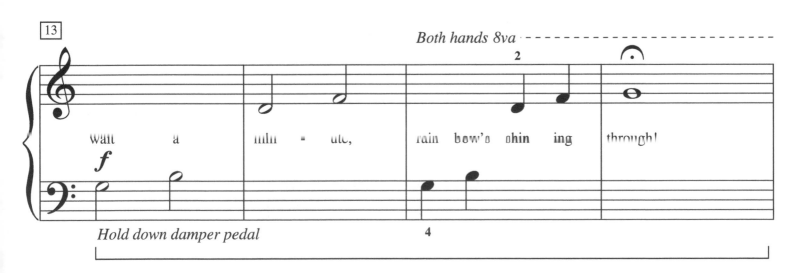

Both hands 8va

wait   a   min   -   ute,   rain   bow's   shin   ing   through!

Hold down damper pedal

But - ter - flies and rain - bows

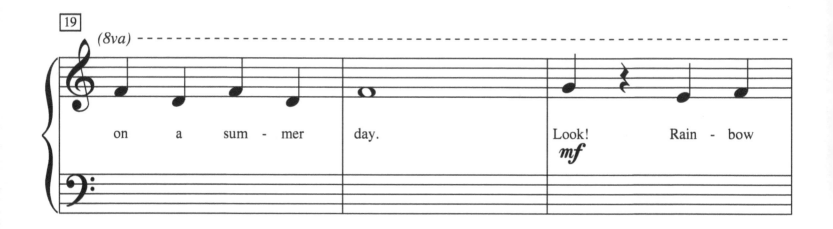

on a sum - mer day. Look! Rain - bow

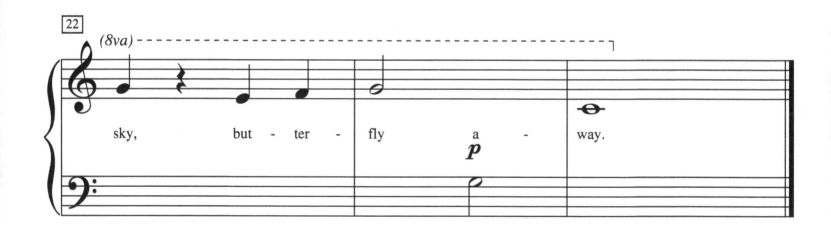

sky, but - ter - fly a - way.

Accidental Wizard

By Phillip Keveren

Accompaniment (Play both hands one octave higher throughout.)

Chill Out!

By Bill Boyd

Fast Rock

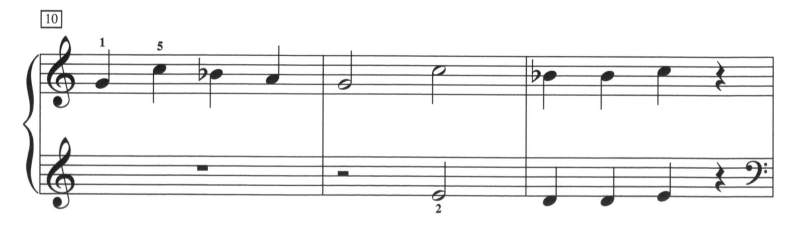

Down by the Lake

Words and Music by
Jennifer Linn

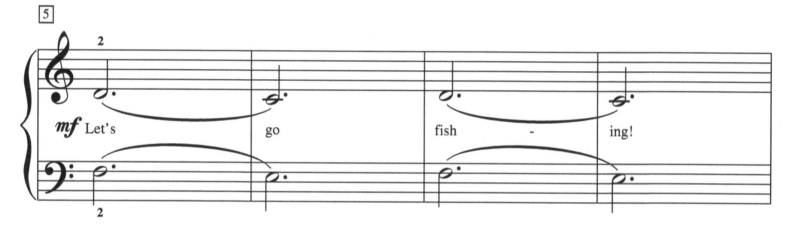

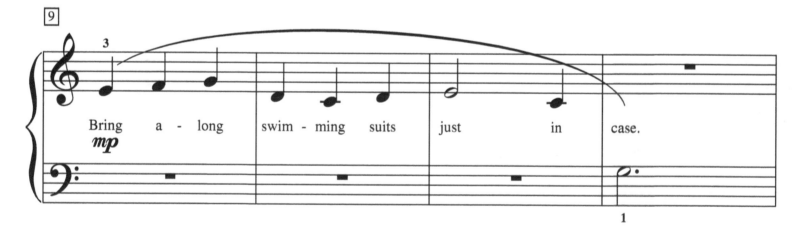

Accompaniment (Student plays one octave higher than written.)

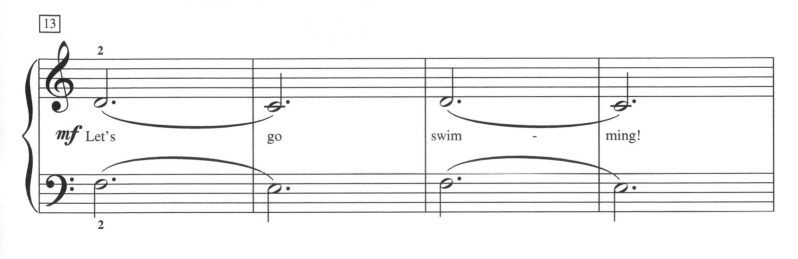

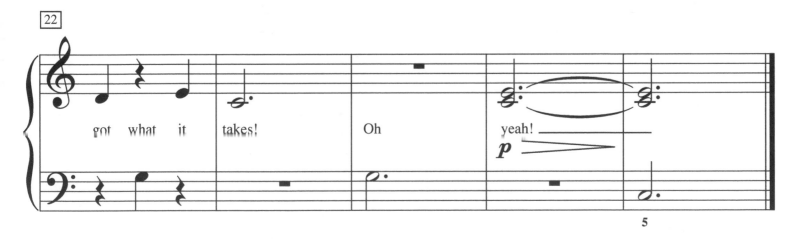

Commissioned by the Wisconsin Music Teachers Association – Greater Milwaukee Chapter

Gone Fishin'

Secondo

By Carol Klose

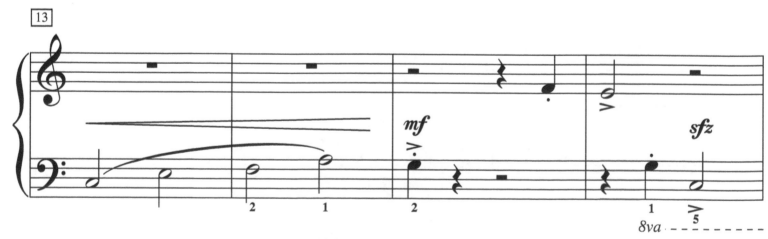

Gone Fishin'

Primo

By Carol Klose

Cheerfully (♩ = 138)

Play both hands one octave higher than written.

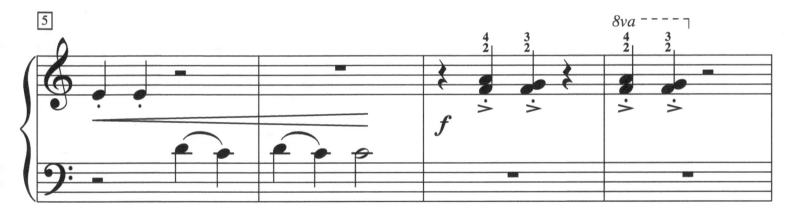

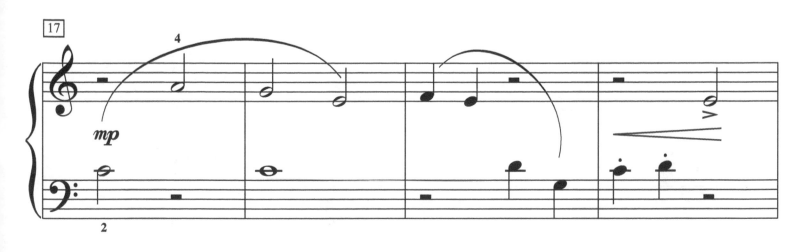

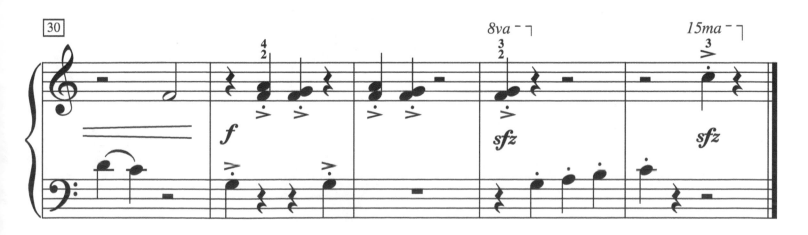

The Merry Merry-Go-Round

Words and Music by
Jennifer Linn

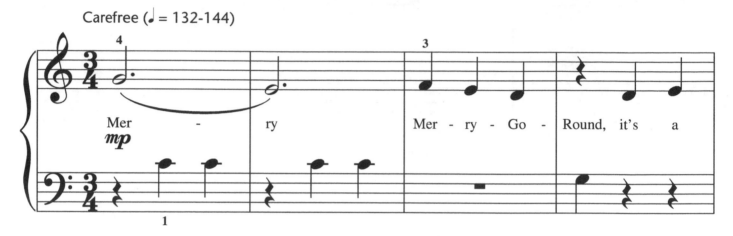

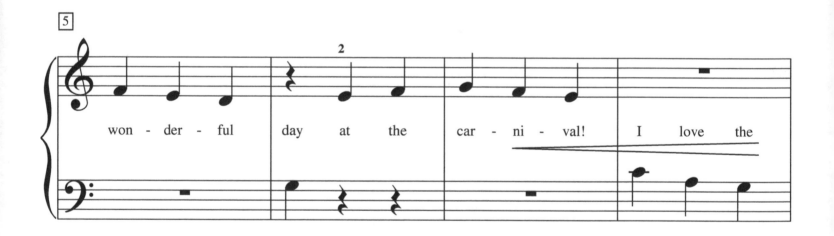

Accompaniment (Student plays one octave higher than written.)

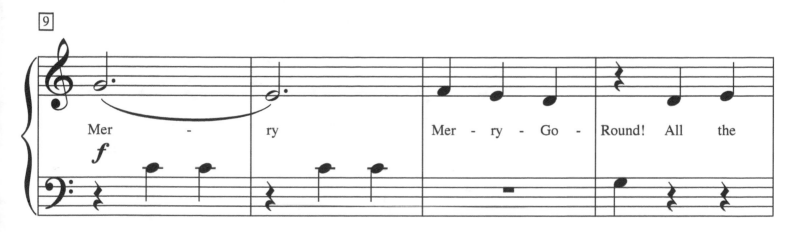

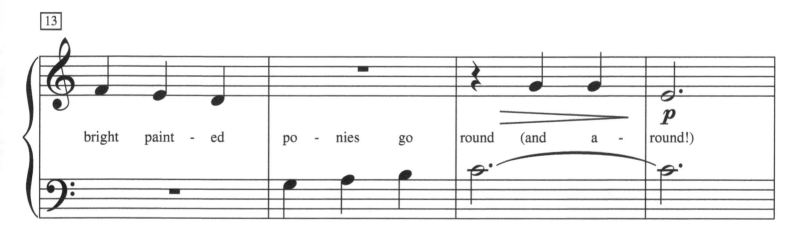

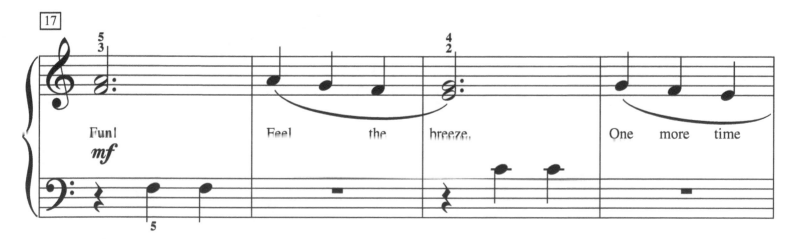

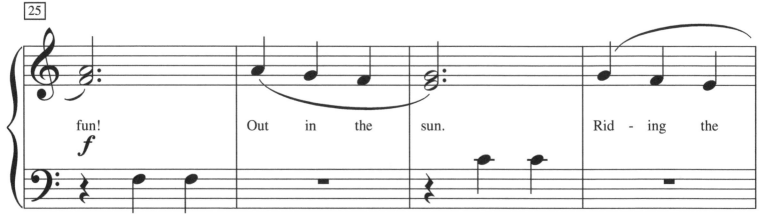

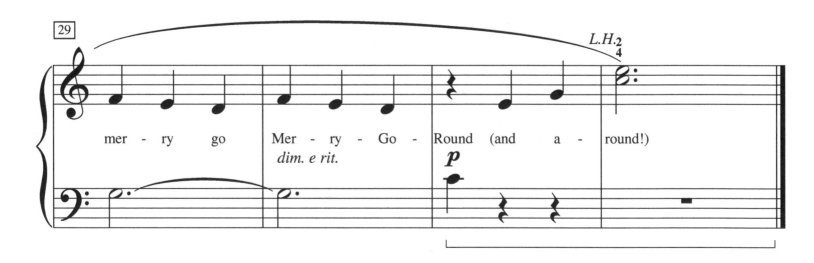

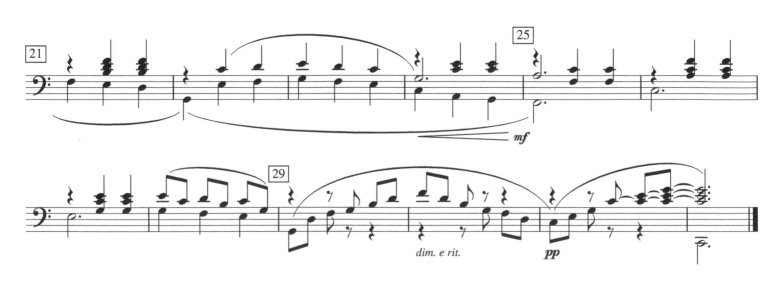

Pink Lemonade

Words and Music by
Jennifer Linn

Carefree (♩ = 100)

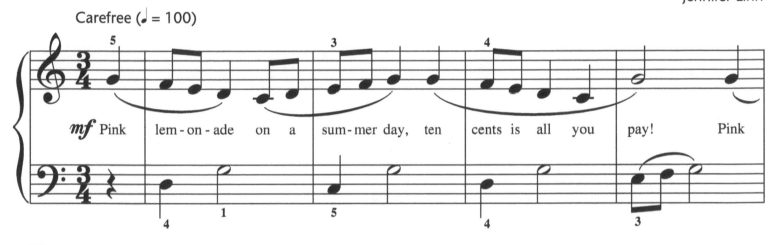

mf Pink lem-on-ade on a sum-mer day, ten cents is all you pay! Pink

lem-on-ade in the sum-mer heat, the taste __ can't be beat!

rit. (2nd time)

Fine

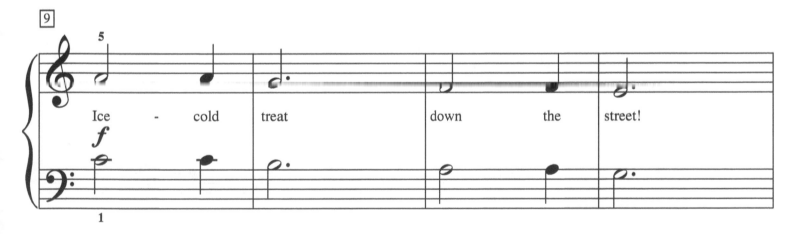

Ice - cold treat down the street!

f

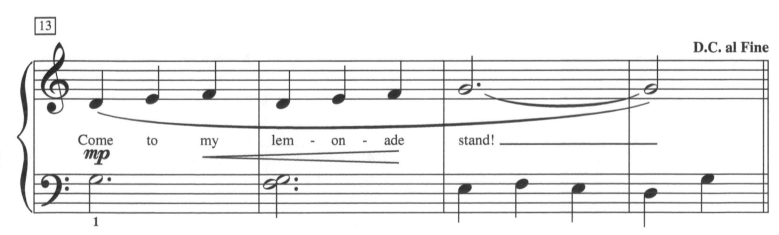

D.C. al Fine

Come to my lem-on-ade stand! _____

mp

Rockin' the Boat

By Bill Boyd

Fast Rock

for Katherine Rose Klose

Teeter-Totter

By Carol Klose

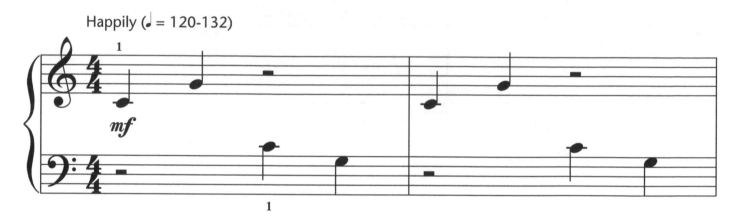

Accompaniment (Student plays one octave higher than written.)

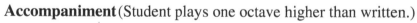

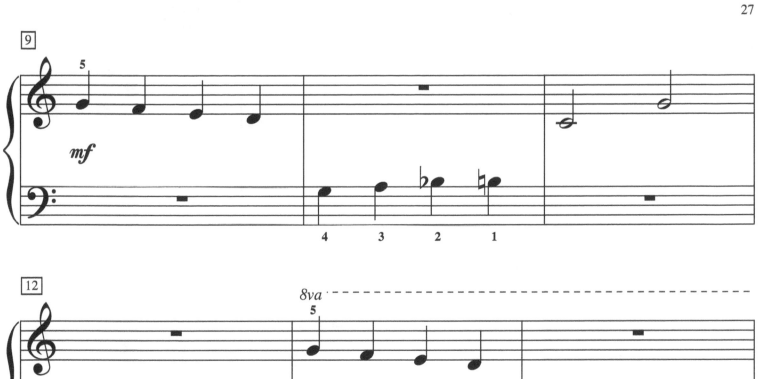

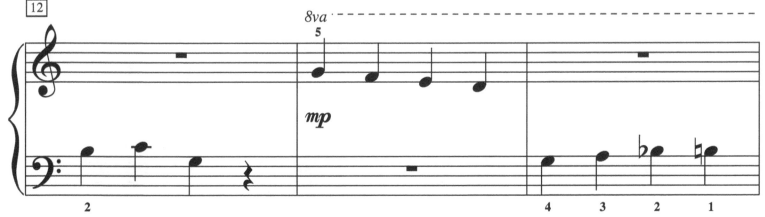

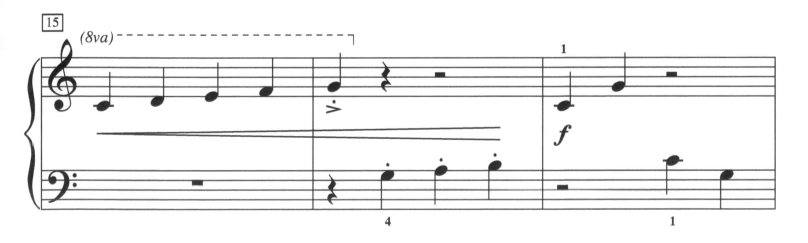

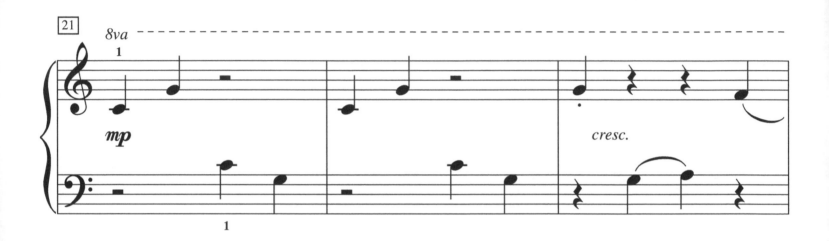

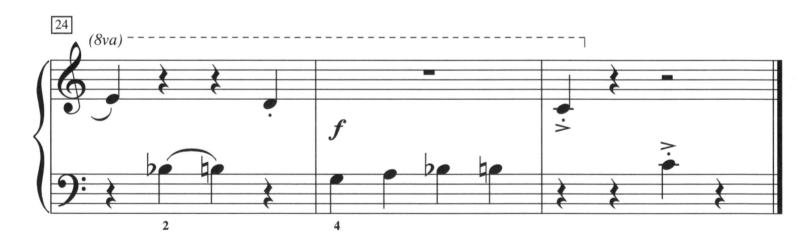

Wind Chimes

By Carol Klose

Flowing, in "two" (♩ = 72)
Play both hands one octave higher throughout.

Hold down damper pedal throughout. (Solo)

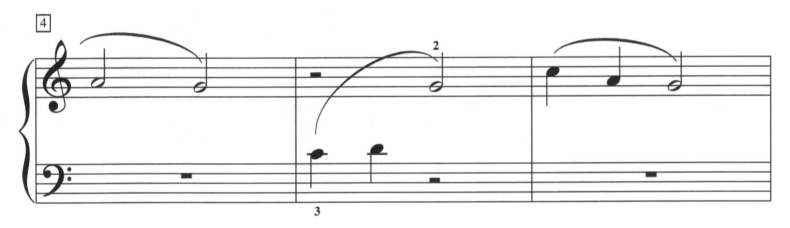

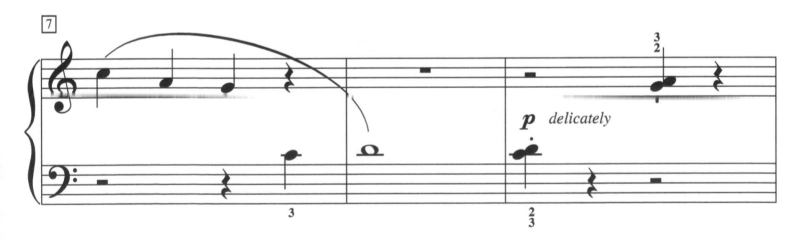

Accompaniment (Student plays one octave higher than written.)

Flowing, in "two" (♩ = 72)

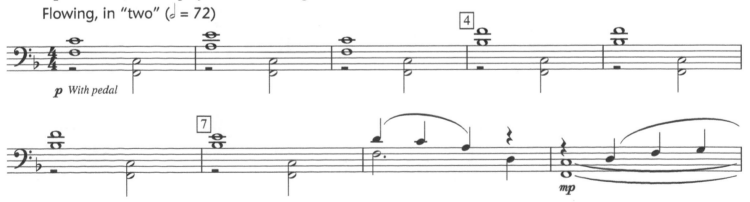

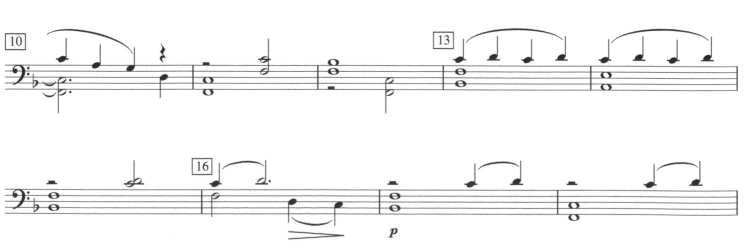

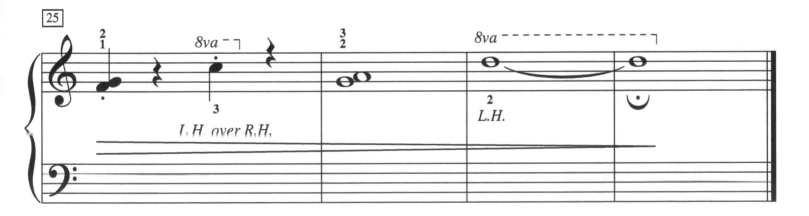

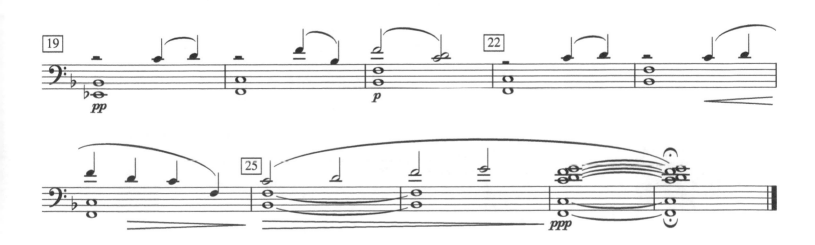

COMPOSER SHOWCASE
HAL·LEONARD STUDENT PIANO LIBRARY

This series showcases great original piano music from our **Hal Leonard Student Piano Library** family of composers. Carefully graded for easy selection.

BILL BOYD

JAZZ BITS (AND PIECES)
Early Intermediate Level
00290312 11 Solos..................$7.99

JAZZ DELIGHTS
Intermediate Level
00240435 11 Solos..................$8.99

JAZZ FEST
Intermediate Level
00240436 10 Solos..................$8.99

JAZZ PRELIMS
Early Elementary Level
00290032 12 Solos..................$7.99

JAZZ SKETCHES
Intermediate Level
00220001 8 Solos..................$8.99

JAZZ STARTERS
Elementary Level
00290425 10 Solos..................$7.99

JAZZ STARTERS II
Late Elementary Level
00290434 11 Solos..................$7.99

JAZZ STARTERS III
Late Elementary Level
00290465 12 Solos..................$8.99

THINK JAZZ!
Early Intermediate Level
00290417 Method Book..................$12.99

TONY CARAMIA

JAZZ MOODS
Intermediate Level
00296728 8 Solos..................$6.95

SUITE DREAMS
Intermediate Level
00296775 4 Solos..................$6.99

SONDRA CLARK

THREE ODD METERS
Intermediate Level
00296472 3 Duets..................$6.95

MATTHEW EDWARDS

CONCERTO FOR YOUNG PIANISTS
FOR 2 PIANOS, FOUR HANDS
Intermediate Level Book/CD
00296356 3 Movements $19.99

CONCERTO NO. 2 IN G MAJOR
FOR 2 PIANOS, 4 HANDS
Intermediate Level Book/CD
00296670 3 Movements..................$17.99

PHILLIP KEVEREN

MOUSE ON A MIRROR
Late Elementary Level
00296361 5 Solos..................$8.99

MUSICAL MOODS
Elementary/Late Elementary Level
00296714 7 Solos..................$6.99

SHIFTY-EYED BLUES
Late Elementary Level
00296374 5 Solos..................$7.99

CAROL KLOSE

THE BEST OF CAROL KLOSE
Early Intermediate to Late Intermediate Level
00146151 15 Solos..................$12.99

CORAL REEF SUITE
Late Elementary Level
00296354 7 Solos..................$7.50

DESERT SUITE
Intermediate Level
00296667 6 Solos..................$7.99

FANCIFUL WALTZES
Early Intermediate Level
00296473 5 Solos..................$7.95

GARDEN TREASURES
Late Intermediate Level
00296787 5 Solos..................$8.50

ROMANTIC EXPRESSIONS
Intermediate/Late Intermediate Level
00296923 5 Solos..................$8.99

WATERCOLOR MINIATURES
Early Intermediate Level
00296848 7 Solos..................$7.99

JENNIFER LINN

AMERICAN IMPRESSIONS
Intermediate Level
00296471 6 Solos..................$8.99

ANIMALS HAVE FEELINGS TOO
Early Elementary/Elementary Level
00147789 8 Solos..................$8.99

CHRISTMAS IMPRESSIONS
Intermediate Level
00296706 8 Solos..................$8.99

JUST PINK
Elementary Level
00296722 9 Solos..................$8.99

LES PETITES IMAGES
Late Elementary Level
00296664 7 Solos..................$8.99

LES PETITES IMPRESSIONS
Intermediate Level
00296355 6 Solos..................$7.99

REFLECTIONS
Late Intermediate Level
00296843 5 Solos..................$8.99

TALES OF MYSTERY
Intermediate Level
00296769 6 Solos..................$8.99

LYNDA LYBECK-ROBINSON

ALASKA SKETCHES
Early Intermediate Level
00119637 8 Solos..................$7.99

AN AWESOME ADVENTURE
Late Elementary Level
00137563..................$7.99

FOR THE BIRDS
Early Intermediate/Intermediate Level
00237078 ....$8.99

WHISPERING WOODS
Late Elementary Level
00275905 9 Solos..................$8.99

MONA REJINO

CIRCUS SUITE
Late Elementary Level
00296665 5 Solos..................$6.99

COLOR WHEEL
Early Intermediate Level
00201951 6 Solos..................$8.99

JUST FOR KIDS
Elementary Level
00296840 8 Solos..................$7.99

MERRY CHRISTMAS MEDLEYS
Intermediate Level
00296799 5 Solos..................$8.99

MINIATURES IN STYLE
Intermediate Level
00148088 6 Solos..................$8.99

PORTRAITS IN STYLE
Early Intermediate Level
00296507 6 Solos..................$8.99

EUGÉNIE ROCHEROLLE

CELEBRATION SUITE
Intermediate Level
00152724 3 Duets (1 Piano, 4 Hands)..............$8.99

**ENCANTOS ESPAÑOLES
(SPANISH DELIGHTS)**
Intermediate Level
00125451 6 Solos..................$8.99

JAMBALAYA
Intermediate Level
00296654 Ensemble (2 Pianos, 8 Hands)........$12.99

JAMBALAYA
Intermediate Level
00296725 Piano Duo (2 Pianos) $7.95

LITTLE BLUES CONCERTO
FOR 2 PIANOS, 4 HANDS
Early Intermediate Level
00142801 Piano Duo (2 Pianos, 4 Hands)........$12.99

TOUR FOR TWO
Late Elementary Level
00296832 6 Duets..................$7.99

TREASURES
Late Elementary/Early Intermediate Level
00296924 7 Solos..................$8.99

JEREMY SISKIND

BIG APPLE JAZZ
Intermediate Level
00278209 8 Solos..................$8.99

MYTHS AND MONSTERS
Late Elementary/Early Intermediate Level
00148148 9 Solos..................$7.99

CHRISTOS TSITSAROS

DANCES FROM AROUND THE WORLD
Early Intermediate Level
00296688 7 Solos..................$8.99

LYRIC BALLADS
Intermediate/Late Intermediate Level
00102404 6 Solos..................$8.99

POETIC MOMENTS
Intermediate Level
00296403 8 Solos..................$8.99

SEA DIARY
Early Intermediate Level
00253486 9 Solos..................$8.99

SONATINA HUMORESQUE
Late Intermediate Level
00296772 3 Movements $6.99

SONGS WITHOUT WORDS
Intermediate Level
00296506 9 Solos..................$9.99

THREE PRELUDES
Early Advanced Level
00130747 ....$8.99

THROUGHOUT THE YEAR
Late Elementary Level
00296723 12 Duets..................$6.95

ADDITIONAL COLLECTIONS

AT THE LAKE
by Elvina Pearce
Elementary/Late Elementary Level
00131642 10 Solos and Duets..................$7.99

COUNTY RAGTIME FESTIVAL
by Fred Kern
Intermediate Level
00296882 7 Rags..................$7.99

LITTLE JAZZERS
by Jennifer Watts
Elementary/Late Elementary Level
00154573 Solos..................8.99

PLAY THE BLUES!
by Luann Carman (Method Book)
Early Intermediate Level
00296357 10 Solos..................$9.99

Prices, contents, and availability subject
to change without notice.

HAL·LEONARD®
www.halleonard.com

0419

144